Heavenly Journey Recipes

Yolanda Armstead

© Copyright 2024 by Yolanda Armstead
All rights reserved.

No part of this book may be reproduced without the expressed permission of the author.

Published by: Dixon Publishing Company
P. O. Box 32023
Aurora, CO 80041

For bulk orders, please contact the publisher at 515-99-BOOKS

Graphic Designer: Dixon Publishing Company
Editor: Tiffany Heflin, Dixon Publishing Company
Press Kit Designer: Aishwary Tiwari
Press Kit: Beatrice Bruno
Interior Designer: Michael Myers, Dixon Publishing Company
Writer: Yolanda Armstead

Table of Contents

After Hours Breakfast Rice 7
Blessed Bling Butter Sauce 9
Mama Joe Shrimp Sauce Piquant 11
Pepae Microwave Pecan Candy 13
Choctaw Pineapple Boat 15
Budget Tamales 17
Mama Joe Melt in Your Mouth Smothered Liver 21
Carnival Time Pig Ears 23
Slap Your Mama Banana Pudding 25
Spinach Crawfish Pasta 27
Choctaw Coconut Fried Catfish 29
Mama Die for Cabbage Rolls 31
Yo's Crab Cakes 35
Yo's Shrimp Stuffed Eggs 37
Yo's Fried Crabs 39
Grandma Catherine's Tea Cakes 41
Turnips and Shrimp 43
Seafood Cornbread Dressing 45
Garlic Butter Shrimp 49
Brother Dee's Bacon-Wrapped Thighs 51
Choctaw Honey-Glazed Ribs 53
Yo's Famous Pecan Praline Brownies 55
Breaking Bread Fried Turkey Wings 57
Shrimp Stuffed Potatoes 59
Seafood Pies 63
Fig Brie 65
Seafood Croquettes 67
Family Legacy 68

After Hours Breakfast Rice

After Hours Breakfast Rice

Ingredients

1 cup crumbled cooked bacon
2 lb hot breakfast sausage
1 small chopped onion
1 half chopped red pepper
1 half chopped green pepper
1/4 cup green onion
2 cups cooked rice
10 oz can of mushroom soup
6 eggs
1 cup of frozen peas
1 cup of shredded cheese (your choice)

Instructions

Beat and scramble eggs and set aside. Brown the sausage in a large skillet, breaking and cutting up as you cook. Drain off the grease, add onion, bell peppers. Cook for about 5 minutes, add soup and stir for about 2 minutes then add rice, peas, cheese and green onions. Saute for 2 more minutes.

Serve and enjoy!

Blessed Bling Butter Sauce

Blessed Bling Butter Sauce

Ingredients

2 cups butter
1/4 cup minced garlic
1 tbsp paprika
½ tsp cayenne pepper
½ tsp black pepper
½ tsp garlic powder
½ tsp onion powder
½ tsp Accent
1 tbsp Tabasco
1 tbsp salt
½ tsp parsley flakes

Instructions

In a microwave bowl, melt butter for about 1 minute.

Add all the spices to butter and mix thoroughly until all spices are mixed and blended well into butter.

Mama Joe Shrimp Sauce Piquant

Mama Joe Shrimp Sauce Piquant

Ingredients

2 pounds crawfish tails
12 crawfish heads
3 tsp of creole seasoning or your favorite
4 tbsp all purpose flour
¾ cup of oil
2 cups chopped onion
1 cup bell pepper
½ cup chopped celery
1/4 cup chopped garlic
2 cups tomato sauce
1 cup of rotel
4 cups seafood stock

Instructions

Clean and season shrimps with favorite seasoning drained well and refrigerate until ready to use.

Heat oil in a stockpot over medium to high heat, stir in the flour and cook stirring constantly until the roux turns medium brown or caramel color. Add in onions, bell peppers, celery until they are tender then add garlic and stir for about 2 minutes.

Add the seafood stock and more seasoning to taste and bring to a boil continue cooking on low to medium heat. Stir for about 5 to 7 more minutes and add tomato sauce and rotel and simmer for about 45 minutes to an hour so that the sauce is completely cooked. Add more stock if needed and add in shrimps. Let simmer for about 15 to 20 minutes.

Serve over rice and enjoy.

Pepae Microwave Pecan Candy

Pepae Microwave Pecan Candy

Ingredients

1 stick of salted butter, no substitute
2 cans sweetened condensed milk (14 ounce)
1 cup brown sugar
2 cups chopped pecans
3 tsp pure vanilla extract

Instructions

Add butter to microwave safe bowl. Melt for 30 seconds.

Combine sugar and sweetened condensed milk in bowl and mix well stirring with spoon.

Microwave on high for about 6 to 7 minutes.

Remove from microwave and stir in pecans, mixing very well.

Return to the microwave for 15 to 17 minutes depending on your microwave. Remove from the microwave, stir well every 3 minutes. (WATCH CAREFULLY IN MICROWAVE, MAKING SURE CANDY DOES NOT BOIL OVER).

At the end of the 15 to 17 minutes, stir in vanilla extract.

Pour or drop onto greased cookie sheet and let cool for 15 minutes and enjoy.

Choctaw Pineapple Boat

Choctaw Pineapple Boat

Ingredients

1 large pineapple
3 tbsp oil
6 boneless chicken thighs cut in cubes
2 tbsp Old Bay seasoning
1 tsp cayenne
2 tbsp soy sauce
1 tbsp brown sugar
1 tbsp minced garlic
½ cup chicken stock
Sesame seeds for garnishing

Instructions

Carefully cut the pineapple in half lengthwise using a sharp knife. Using the knife tip, cut around the inside edge of the pineapple being careful NOT to cut through the pineapple piercing a hole.

Slice down and across the pineapple then scoop out the pineapple cubes with a spoon. Discard the core and keep the rest of the pineapple set aside.

In a large pan, heat the oil over medium heat. Add cut up chicken and season with Old Bay and pepper. Saute until browned and cooked thoroughly. Remove the chicken and set aside.

In the same pot, add the cubed pineapple, soy sauce, brown sugar, garlic and cook for a few minutes. Stir in the chicken stock to a boil then simmer, stirring occasionally until the sauce has reduced and thickened.

Add chicken back to pan and stir until evenly coated with sauce. Serve in the empty pineapple halves with some rice. Garnish with sesame seeds.

Budget Tamales

Budget Tamales

Ingredients

2 lb ground beef
½ finely chopped small onion
½ finely chopped small green bell pepper
1 tsp minced garlic
¼ cup chili powder
1 tbsp garlic powder
1 tbsp onion powder
¼ cup paprika
1 tbsp cayenne pepper or to taste
Tony Chachere's or creole seasoning to taste
2 cups chicken stock
2-28 oz cans Enchilada sauce
12 medium dried corn husks (soak in cold water until ready to use)

Preparing the Meal Dough
3 cups masa harina (dried masa flour for tamales)
2 tbsp salt
2 tbsp baking powder
Pork lard melted (as needed)
Water as needed

Instructions

Preheat oven 375 degrees

In a saucepan add ground beef, onions, bell peppers, minced garlic, chili powder, garlic powder, onion powder, cayenne pepper and Tony Chachere's to taste. Cook on medium heat and saute until beef is completely cooked. Add 1 cup of enchilada sauce, turn off heat and let cool.

While the filling is cooling. Prepare meal dough in a large bowl. Pour masa, salt, baking powder, and mix well. Slowly add melted pork lard

Continued…

a little at a time, mixing until soft dough forms and is easy to spread. If the meal starts to dry out, stir in 2 tbsp of water.

Remove husk from water and shake off water. Lay the husk flat on the pan and spread the desired amount of meal dough thinly (but make sure there is enough meal on the husk) from the edge to the center of the husk. Leaving ¼ inch from top to bottom of the husk clear, spoon meat filling in the center of the tamale in a roll like a cigar.

Taking close to you, fold over the middle of the tamale and continue to roll like a cigar. Take the bottom of the tamale and fold it close to the bottom and place it side down in a baking dish. Continue the process until all tamales are rolled and done.

In a large bowl add 2 cans of enchiladas sauce, 1 cup water, paprika and seasoning to taste and mix well. Pour over the tamales. Cover with foil and bake for 1 ½ hour or until sauce thickens.

Cool and serve.

Enjoy!

Mama Joe Melt in Your Mouth Smothered Liver

Mama Joe Melt in Your Mouth Smothered Liver

Ingredients

1-16 oz pack of frozen calf liver (sliced), semi-thawed when ready to cook
¼ cup of Tony Chachere's
1 tsp garlic powder
1 tsp onion powder
1 tsp cayenne pepper
1 tbsp Accent
2 cups all purpose flour
Oil
1 tbsp Kitchen Bouquet
1 cup chopped season blend

Instructions

Semi-thaw liver and remove from package one at a time. Combine Tony Chachere's, garlic powder, onion powder, cayenne pepper, and Accent in a bowl. Season liver on both sides with combined seasoning. Place each piece of liver one at a time in flour, dusting well on both sides.

In a large deep skillet, add 1 cup of oil. Heat on medium heat. When oil is hot, place the floured liver into skillet. Lightly brown on both sides for only 2 to 3 minutes, no more. Liver will still have blood in it.

After all the liver is lightly browned, remove from pan and add seasoning blend. Sauté for about 5 minutes until tender and fragrant. Replace liver in pan and add 1½ cups of water. Add more seasoning to taste and 1 tbsp of Kitchen Bouquet. Let simmer for about 5 more minutes. Turn off heat. Keep covered for 5 more minutes. Serve over grits, potatoes, or rice.

Carnival Tyme Pig Ears

Carnival Time Pig Ears

Ingredients

- 1-10 count pack small, thin flour tortilla shells (20-oz size)
- 4 cups Oil
- 1 cup cinnamon sugar
- 8 oz. Steen syrup
- 6 oz. chopped pecans

Instructions

In a frying pan, heat oil to 350 degrees. Place the tortilla shell in oil carefully. Once the shell puffs up, hold shell down in the middle with a potato masher until golden brown on both sides and the shell is crispy, forming a funny shape. Remove shell and place on paper towel to drain. Repeat the process until all shells are fried.

Pour syrup into a medium bowl. Place shells on a baking sheet. Apply syrup with a pastry brush to each shell thickly. Sprinkle with pecans and cinnamon sugar. Let sit for 5 minutes. Enjoy.

Wrap each pig ear individually in cling wrap.

Slap Your Mama Banana Pudding

Slap Your Mama Banana Pudding

Ingredients

1/3 cup all-purpose flour
3 cups whole milk
¼ tsp salt
4 eggs separated
2 tbsp butter
2 tbsp vanilla extract

1 tbsp almond extract
5 ½ oz. Vanilla wafer cookies
5 bananas cut into ¼" slices
1 1/2 cups sugar
5 tbsp sugar

Topping
2 cups heavy whipping cream
4 tbsp sugar
1 tbsp vanilla

Instructions

Place a medium metal bowl in the freezer until pudding is ready.

In a large saucepan, combine 1 ½ cups of sugar, flour, and salt. In a bowl, whisk together the milk and egg yolks only. Then combine the milk and sugar mixture together in a saucepan, whisking it thoroughly until it's smooth.

Place the saucepan with mixture on medium heat for 10 minutes, whisking constantly until mixture is very thick (timing may vary 10 to 15 minutes).

Remove from heat and add butter, vanilla and almond extract. Stir. Layer bottom of a quart glass baking dish with vanilla wafers, sliced bananas, and half of the pudding mix. Continue and repeat layers.

Take the metal bowl out of the freezer and add heavy whipping cream, sugar, and vanilla. Whisk until cream is stiff. Add crumbled vanilla wafers on top. Add wafers to decorate pudding and serve.

Spinach Crawfish Pasta

Spinach Crawfish Pasta

Ingredients

- 1 lb crawfish tails
- ¼ cup butter
- 2 tbsp minced garlic
- 1 small onion, chopped finely
- ½ small green bell pepper, chopped finely
- ½ small red bell pepper, chopped finely
- 2 celery ribs, chopped finely
- 1 tbsp garlic powder
- 1 tsp Accent
- Tony Chachere's to taste
- 1 10 oz can cream of celery soup
- 1 tbsp cayenne pepper
- 1 lb box of fettuccine noodles or your favorite pasta, cooked to package directions
- 1 ½ cups of fresh spinach
- 1 ½ cups of heavy cream
- 6 oz jalapeno cream cheese

Instructions

Set oven to 350 degrees.

In a small Dutch oven, add butter and sauté onion, bell peppers, and celery. Cook until soft and caramelized. Add minced garlic and cook until fragrant, about 2 minutes. Add crawfish and cook until heated thoroughly.

Add heavy cream and jalapeno cream cheese. Cook until cream cheese is melted. Add your favorite Creole seasoning to taste. Fold in fresh spinach.

Add prepared pasta mix and reduce heat to medium or low. Cook until sauce lightly thickens. Garnish with parmesan cheese. Eat and enjoy.

Choctaw Coconut Fried Catfish

Choctaw Coconut Fried Catfish

Ingredients

2 cups all-purpose flour
6 catfish filets
⅓ cup Old Bay seasoning
3 large eggs
¾ cup milk
1 tbsp lemon juice
1 ½ cups sweetened coconut flakes
1 ½ cups panko
1 tsp garlic powder
1 tsp onion powder
1 tbsp Old Bay seasoning
¼ tsp black pepper oil

Instructions

Wash and season fish with ⅓ cup of Old Bay seasoning.

In a bowl, whisk eggs, lemon juice and milk together and set aside.

In another shallow bowl, stir and combine flour, coconut, panko, 1 tbsp Old Bay seasoning, pepper, garlic powder, onion powder.

In a large skillet, pour oil and heat over medium heat.

Working in batches, dip fish into egg batter then into flour mixture, shaking off excess. Once oil is heated to about 350 degrees for deep frying, carefully place battered fish into hot oil and deep fry until golden brown, approximately 2 minutes, turning occasionally.

Remove fish from oil with a slotted spoon and let drain on paper towels. Let cool, serve, and enjoy!

Mama Die for Cabbage Rolls

Mama Die for Cabbage Rolls

Ingredients

2 lbs ground beef
12 large cabbage leaves (no tears or holes) You can buy just the leaves at the grocery store, instead of the whole cabbage.
1 cup of chopped seasoning blend
3 tbsp parsley flakes
2 eggs

1 cup uncooked rice
1 tsp Accent
2 tbsp cayenne
2 tbsp garlic powder
1 tsp onion powder
¾ cups of Tony Chacheres
½ cup of garlic herb pasta sauce
24 toothpicks

Sauce
24 oz Hunt's garlic herb pasta sauce
10 oz can of Rotel
1 cup of water

1 tbsp Accent
1 tbsp onion powder
3 tbsp salt
2 tbsp chili powder
1 tbsp sugar

Instructions

Preheat the oven to 350 degrees. Combine ground meat, seasoning blend, parsley flakes, eggs, rice, Accent, cayenne, garlic powder, onion powder, Tony Chachere's, ½ cup pasta sauce. With hands, mix ingredients thoroughly together and set aside.

Boil cabbage leaves for about 2 minutes until soft but still a little tender. Leaves should be easy to handle but not fall apart. Remove leaves carefully from hot water and set aside to cool.

Take cabbage leaves and remove any thick stems. Lay the cabbage leaf flat and add ¼ cup of filling to the center of the leaf. Fold in the sides and roll the cabbage up. Insert toothpick to keep the cabbage roll from opening and place seam with toothpick down in a deep baking pan. Repeat until all cabbage rolls are done.

Combine all ingredients for the sauce in a large bowl. Once done mixing, pour over the cabbage rolls covering them completely. Add more water to the pan if needed. You can also add more seasoning to taste.

Cover tightly with foil and bake for about 1 ½ hours. Let cool before serving and enjoy.

Be Blessed!

Yo's Crab Cakes

Yo's Crab Cakes

Ingredients

1 pound lump crab meat
1 large egg
2 tsp Worcestershire sauce
2 tsp Old Bay seasoning
2 tbsp crab boil
⅓ cup mayonnaise
1 ½ tsp yellow mustard
2 tbsp parsley flakes
1 cup butter crumbled bread crumbs
Oil for frying

Instructions

Combine the crab, egg, Old Bay seasoning, Worcestershire sauce, mayonnaise, mustard, crab boil, and ⅔ cups of breadcrumbs together. Form into 6 crab cakes. Roll them into tight balls and then gently smash down forming a patty.

Place each crab cake into breadcrumbs coating them, then place on a cookie sheet. In a large frying pan on medium heat, once oil is hot, add the crab cakes and cook for about 4 minutes on each side until golden brown. Cook completely.

Remove crab cakes from oil. Set aside on a paper towel and let drain. Enjoy and eat with your favorite sauce.

Yo's Shrimp Stuffed Eggs

Yo's Shrimp Stuffed Eggs

Ingredients

1 lb cooked salad shrimp (thawed)
8 boiled eggs (peeled)
¾ cup mayonnaise
1/2 stick real butter
3 tbsp yellow mustard
1 tsp black pepper
1 tbsp parsley flakes
1 tsp garlic powder
1 tsp onion powder
2 tbsp Tony Chachere's
1 tbsp sugar

Instructions

Cut the eggs in half lengthwise. Carefully remove the yolks and place in a bowl.

With the back of a fork, smash the egg yolks, mayonnaise, and sugar until smooth. Set aside in a skillet. Melt butter on medium heat. Add shrimp. Toss in butter. Add black pepper, parsley, garlic powder, onion powder, Tony Chachere's and sauté for 2 to 3 minutes. Remove from heat. Take out 16 sauteed shrimp and set aside for garnishing. Take remaining shrimp and egg mixture. Fill the egg white halves with the stuffing mix and place one sauteed shrimp on top of each egg.

Garnish with parsley and paprika. Serve and enjoy.

Yo's Fried Crabs

Yo's Fried Crabs

Ingredients

6 large live crabs
2 cups Blessed Bling Butter Sauce
Oil for deep fryer

Liquid Batter
1 tbsp black pepper
1 tbsp salt
2 cup milk
3 eggs beaten
(Mix all ingredients together in bowl and set aside)

Seasoned Flour
3 cups flour
2 tbsp black pepper
2 tbsp salt
1 cup paprika
1 tbsp garlic powder
1 tbsp onion powder
(Mix all ingredients together and set aside)

Instructions

Wash crabs, then place in freezer for about 2 hours to put them to sleep. Prep the liquid batter and seasoned flour while the crabs are in the freezer. After 2 hours, take crabs out of the freezer. Take off the top shell of the crab and clean, then chop in half.

Place crabs in a large bowl and pour butter sauce over them. Then dredge crabs in seasoned flour. Dip in the liquid batter and then dredge in seasoned flour again. Deep fry in hot oil until cooked and golden brown.

Grandma Cat's Tea Cakes

Grandma Catherine's Tea Cakes

Ingredients

3 cups all-purpose flour
1 ½ cups of sugar
2 eggs
½ tsp baking soda
½ tsp salt
¼ tsp nutmeg
2 tsp vanilla extract
1 tsp butter extract

Instructions

In a medium bowl, add together butter and sugar and stir into a smooth cream. Beat in the eggs one at a time, then stir in the vanilla. Combine the flour, baking soda, salt, and nutmeg stirring into a dough. Knead dough for a few minutes on a flour board until smooth. Cover and put in the refrigerator until firm.

Preheat the oven to 325 degrees on a lightly floured surface and roll dough out into ¼ inch thickness. Cut into ¼ inch square then roll into a ball and place on a cookie sheet 1 ½ inches apart.

Bake for 8 to 10 minutes. Allow to cool on a baking sheet for at least 5 minutes before placing on a wire rack to cool completely.

Turnips and Shrimp

Turnips and Shrimp

Ingredients

5 turnips (peeled, cut in 4 to 6 cubes)
1 lb shrimp (medium/large)
½ cup onion chopped
½ cup green bell peppers
½ cup fresh parsley
2 tbsp Tony Chachere's seasoning
1 tsp cayenne pepper
1 tsp granulated garlic
1 tsp onion powder
1 tsp Accent
¾ cup of sugar
¾ cup of oil
1 ½ cups water
2 tbsp white vinegar

Instructions

Place turnips, vinegar, onions, bell peppers, and seasonings in a pot with water over medium heat and simmer until turnips are tender and water has almost evaporated. Stir in the oil, sugar, and green onion until turnips start to brown. Then add shrimp and a little water if needed. Stir constantly until shrimp are pink and turnips are a nice brown. Serve and enjoy.

Seafood Cornbread Dressing

Seafood Cornbread Dressing

Ingredients

4 boxes of Jiffy cornbread mix (Follow instructions on box and bake.)
2 packs of crawfish tails
10 to 12 oz of lump crab meat
1 pound of shrimp
2 cups butter
3 teaspoons cayenne pepper
1 tsp granulated onion powder
1 tsp granulated garlic powder
2 Tbsp Old Bay seasoning (Add more to your taste)
1 cup of parsley flakes
3 stalks chopped celery
½ onion chopped
2 cloves of garlic, chopped
1 large bell pepper, chopped
3 cups of seafood stock
12 oz can of Carnation milk
5 eggs (beaten)

Instructions

Crumble cooked cornbread while the oven is heating at 350 degrees. Set crumbled cornbread aside. In a large pot, melt butter on medium heat. Add cayenne, onion powder, garlic powder, and a tablespoon of Old Bay seasoning to butter and cook for about 5 minutes to fragrance.

Add chopped celery, onions, garlic, and bell peppers to pot cooking until vegetables are tender and caramelized in seasoning. Add seafood broth. Bring to a boil and then remove from heat. Slowly stir in crumbled cornbread, Carnation milk and eggs until the batter is uniform.

Add shrimp, crabmeat, and crawfish to dressing (I like a lot of seafood in my dressing at every bite, so you can add more seafood if you desire). Add Old Bay or Tony Chachere's to the dressing. Mix thoroughly until well incorporated. Spread into the desired pan and bake uncovered for about 45 minutes to an hour until dressing is golden brown and firm to touch. Serve and enjoy.

Garlic Butter Shrimp

Garlic Butter Shrimp

Ingredients

1 lb medium to large shrimp
4 tbsp of butter
1 tbsp of Old Bay seasoning
3 tbsp of minced garlic
1 lemon freshly squeezed (remove seeds)
1 tbsp of honey
1 tbsp of parsley flakes

Instructions

Place butter in a large skillet and melt over medium heat. Add the shrimp and Old Bay seasoning. Cook for about 5 minutes, stirring occasionally until the shrimp are pink. Add the garlic and honey and cook for one more minute only. Turn off heat. Stir in lemon juice and parsley and serve.

This dish can be served with tacos, salad, baked potatoes, over steak or whatever you desire to enjoy it with.

Brother Dee's Bacon Wrapped Thighs

Brother Dee's Bacon-Wrapped Thighs

Ingredients

8 boneless chicken thighs
16 slices bacon
1 cup brown sugar
2 tbsp cayenne pepper
2 tbsp granulated garlic powder
2 tbsp granulated onion powder
¾ cup of Old Bay seasoning
¾ tsp yellow mustard

Instructions

Preheat oven to 375 degrees. In a bowl, mix all dry ingredients together. Wash thighs and baste with mustard. Sprinkle half the dry ingredients over the thighs and rub together.

Wrap each chicken thigh in 2 slices of bacon. Place the thigh seam side down in a baking pan. When you finish wrapping all the thighs, sprinkle the remaining brown sugar mix over the chicken and bake for 30 minutes or until bacon is crispy and chicken is completely cooked. Baste the chicken occasionally throughout the cooking process with the pan drippings.

If you want your bacon to be a little crispier, cook a little longer. Eat and enjoy.

Choctaw Honey-Glazed Ribs

Choctaw Honey-Glazed Ribs

Ingredients

2 racks of baby back ribs
2 tsp of liquid smoke
¾ cup of yellow mustard
2 tsp of paprika
1 cup of crushed garlic
2 tsp of cayenne pepper
½ cup of Old Bay seasoning
1 small orange (freshly squeezed, remove seeds)
⅓ cup of oil (your choice)
¾ cup of brown sugar
1 cup of honey

Instructions

Prep and wash the ribs. Preheat the oven to 375 degrees. Mix all ingredients together in a large bowl. Place the ribs on a large roaster fitted with a rack and then brush the glaze all over the ribs completely on both sides, making sure the ribs are well basted using all the glaze.

Add ½ inch of water to the bottom of the pan and place in the oven. Bake for about one hour. Every 20 minutes, baste the ribs with drippings from the pan. If the ribs start to cook and brown too fast, cover with foil and lower temperature to 300 degrees until finished cooking.

Let the ribs rest for about 10 minutes before serving so the glaze sticks to the ribs. Enjoy!

Yo's Famous Pecan Praline Brownies

Yo's Famous Pecan Praline Brownies

Ingredients

2 boxes of fudge brownie mix

Praline
6 tbsp of salted butter
1 ½ cups brown sugar
½ cup 2% milk
1 ½ cups powdered sugar
1 tbsp vanilla extract
1 cup chopped pecans
9-inch glass baking dish

Instructions

Preheat the oven to 350 degrees. Spray baking dish with butter cooking spray. Make brownie mix according to directions on the box. Make sure brownies are completely cooled before applying the praline on top.

In a medium saucepan, mix milk, butter, and brown sugar. Cook over medium heat until it comes to a boil. Cook for 2 more minutes making sure you stir constantly. Remove praline mix from heat and stir in pecans, powdered sugar, and vanilla. Stir and let cool for 5 minutes. While cooling, continue to stir. After cooling for 5 minutes, pour mixture over the brownies.

Allow to stand for 30 minutes, then cut into desired squares.

Breaking Bread Fried Turkey Wings

Breaking Bread Fried Turkey Wings

Ingredients

2 lbs turkey wings
2 Tbsp vinegar
1 cup chopped seasoning blend
¾ cup Tony Chachere's
2 tbsp cayenne pepper
2 tbsp granulated garlic
2 tbsp granulated onion

1 cup yellow mustard
4 cups flour
1 cup corn meal
24 oz. oil (enough to cover wings)
Large sheet pan
Large frying pan or deep fryer

Instructions

Wash and season turkey wings in a pot and add chopped seasoning blend, Tony Chachere's, cayenne pepper, garlic, and granulated onions. Boil the wings until they are tender but firm (You do not want wings to fall apart.) After the wings are boiled, drain water and place wings on a sheet pan. Chill until completely cool.

Mix mustard, 1 tbsp cayenne pepper, 2 tbsp Tony Chachere's together. Baste turkey wings with mustard mixture. Heat oil to 375°. **Important:** Make sure the pot is large and deep enough to submerge turkey parts completely into oil.

Mix corn meal, flour, and Old Bay seasoning together in a large zip lock. Place the turkey parts in mixture and shake well until covered completely. Place in hot oil and fry wings until they are crispy and golden brown. After they are cooked, place on paper towel sheet pan to drain and enjoy.

Shrimp Stuffed Potatoes

Shrimp Stuffed Potatoes

Ingredients

6 large baking potatoes
2 sticks of salted butter
Crab boil
4 fresh green onions (separate in half)
1 lb peeled crawfish tails
1 cup chopped onion top
Old Bay seasoning
Sour cream
Shredded cheddar cheese
Black pepper
Granulated garlic oil
Baking pan
Spoon
Large bowl

Instructions

Rub the baked potatoes with olive oil and place on a baking sheet. Place in the oven on a middle rack for 1 hour or until potatoes are soft and tender at 400 degrees. Let potatoes cool completely before scooping.

Suggestion: Baking the potatoes a day before and refrigerating overnight give the best results and will help with faster processing. This will help the potatoes to be firm so you can handle them better and scoop out the potato from the shell without breakage.

After removing the potatoes from the refrigerator, cut the tops of the potatoes long way like a boat. Do not cut in half, only cut the top. After cutting all the potatoes, scoop them into a bowl being careful not to break the shells of the potatoes. Set the shells aside on a flat pan. Do not set on top of one another.

(Continued)

In a pan, add crawfish, and ½ stick of butter with Old Bay seasoning. Sauté for 10 minutes.

Take potatoes that were scooped out of the shell. Add 1 ½ sticks of melted butter, Old Bay, 3 tbsp garlic, 3 tbsp black pepper, fresh green onion, and 3 tbsp crab boil. Mash together. Add crawfish, 1 cup sour cream, 2 cups of shredded cheese and mix together. Spoon mix into the shell. Make a mound at the top of the potato and add more shredded cheese on top. Bake until the cheese melts and serve.

Seafood Pies

Seafood Pies

Ingredients

2 cans of lump crab meat (drained)
1 pack of crawfish tails (drained)
1 pack of frozen cooked shrimp (thaw and drain)
Sour cream
Shredded Mexican cheese
2 medium diced tomatoes
½ stick of butter
Sliced Jalapeno pepper
1 small chopped onion
Parsley flakes
1 pack of thin tortilla shells (20 count)

Instructions

Combine crab meat, crawfish, and shrimp in a saucepan. Add butter and Old Bay seasoning. Sauté on medium heat for about 5 minutes. Remove from heat and add remaining ingredients. Let cool.

While cooling... separate 4 egg yolks from whites. Set aside.

Open tortilla shells placing 10 shells for 20 seconds in the microwave. Place shells on parchment paper. Put one scoop of seafood mix in the middle of the shell, leaving edges clear. With a pastry brush, spread egg yolk around the edges of the shell, then fold top of shell over ingredients and other half of shell over the top of the folded shell. Now fold each side of the shell making a square pie. When finished, place the pie upside down on a cookie sheet until ready to fry. Continue this process until all pies are folded. When all pies are folded, heat oil on medium and fry pies on both sides without sticking them until they are lightly brown. Let cool and serve.

Fig Brie

Fig Brie

Ingredients

1 sheet frozen puff pastry
1/2 cup of fig preserves (Or any desired fruit filling)
3 tbsp of chopped pecans
8 oz brie cheese
1 egg white (lightly beaten with fork)

Instructions

1. Unfold pastry on lightly floured surface
2. Preheat to 350 degrees
3. Roll out pastry to length of ruler into a 12-inch square
4. Cut off sides of pastry and spread fig in the middle of pastry leaving 1 to 2 inches of edges clear. Sprinkle chopped pecans over filling. Place brie in center on top of the pecans then brush exposed pastry sheet with egg white.
5. Fold up edges of pastry over the center of brie and slightly twist together. Make sure the brie is covered completely; this is to ensure that everything stays in the pastry. Make sure to pinch pastry edges. You can use scrap pieces to fill gaps or decorate the top of pastry before baking.
6. Lightly brush the top of the pastry with egg white. Place in the oven on the middle rack until golden brown.

Seafood Croquettes

Seafood Croquettes

Ingredients

- 1 can of salmon
- Lump crab meat
- 1 bag small cooked shrimp (thawed and drained)
- 1 pack crawfish tails (thawed and drained)
- 2 medium boiled potatoes
- 2 eggs
- 1 stick of melted salted butter
- Yellow cornmeal
- All-purpose flour
- Old Bay seasoning
- Liquid crab boil
- ½ small onion (chopped)
- Medium frying pan
- Large mixing bowl
- Oil
- Ice cream scoop
- Parchment paper
- Large cookie sheet

Instructions

In a food chopper or on a cutting board, mix shrimp and crawfish together and chop with a knife. Add in a large bowl with salmon, potato, and crab meat and mix well together. Add 2 eggs, Old Bay seasoning, chopped onions, melted butter and crab boil. Fold together until all ingredients are mixed well together and form a wet ball.

Mix flour and cornmeal together in a bowl. Scoop out mix into your hand and flatten into thick patties. Put patties into the meal. Mix and cover completely on both sides and place on parchment paper covered cookie sheets. Once all patties are done, heat oil on medium and fry brown on both sides turning slowly so croquettes don't break. Let cool and eat. Serve with tartar sauce, green salad or fries.

Family Legacy

Family Legacy

Family Legacy

Family Legacy

Family Legacy

Family Legacy

Family Legacy

Family Legacy

Family Legacy

Made in the USA
Columbia, SC
12 October 2024